HOW TO SURVIVE

in a

DESERT

Written by
Anita Ganeri

Illustrated by
Rob Shone

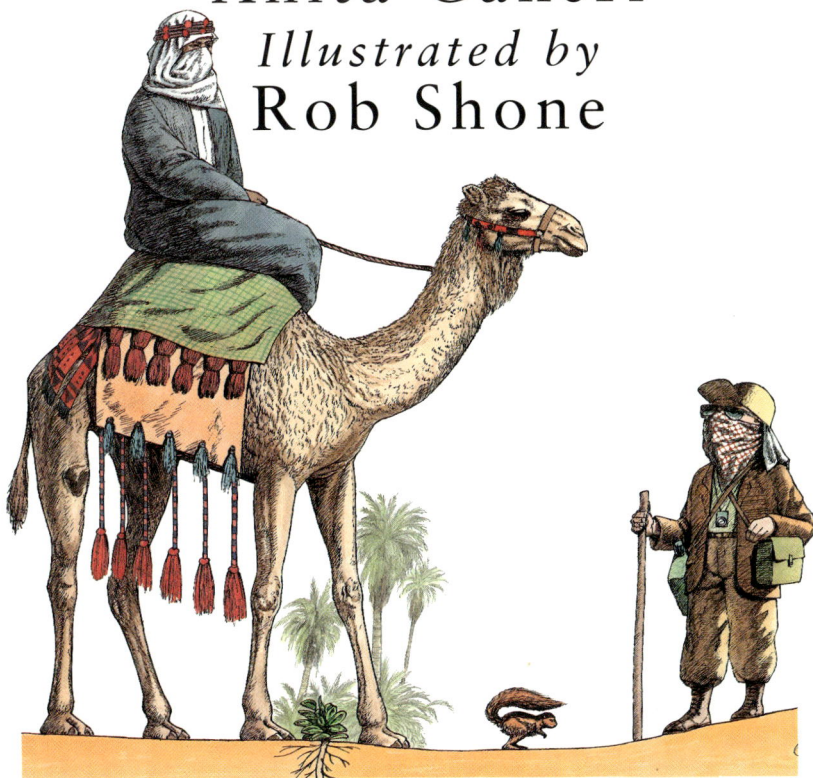

SIMON & SCHUSTER
YOUNG BOOKS

About the author: **Anita Ganeri** has written and edited over 50 books for children, mainly on natural history and the natural world. She has travelled widely and has just returned from a trip to the jungles of Madagascar.

About the consultant: **Antony Mason** is a travel writer and author of books for children on geography and exploration. In the course of his travels, he has visited jungles in South–east Asia, South America and the Caribbean.

About the survival expert: **John Fisher** has served with the British Army Special Forces for 25 years and is trained in survival techniques for jungle and desert terrains. He has personal experience of surviving in the jungles of Malaysia.

Of Australia's 257,000 Aboriginal and Torres Strait Islander people, less than half now live in outback settlements and maintain traditional customs and practices. For the purposes of this book, the term Aborigine applies to these people.

Copyright © S•W Books 1993

Designed and conceived by
S•W Books
28 Percy Street
London W1P 9FF

First published in Great Britain in 1993 by
Simon & Schuster Young Books
Campus 400
Maylands Avenue
Hemel Hempstead
Herts HP2 7EZ

Printed and bound in Belgium by
PROOST International Book Production

British Library Cataloguing in Publication Data available

ISBN 0 7500 1365 6
ISBN 0 7500 1366 4(pb)

CONTENTS

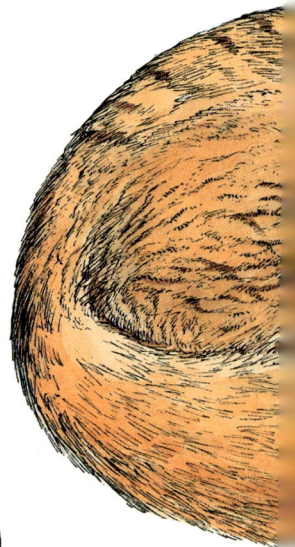

INTRODUCTION

You're hot, tired and very, very thirsty. What's more, you're surrounded by sand as far as the eye can see. What would you do if you suddenly found yourself in the middle of a desert? Would you know where to look for water or how to build a shelter from the sun? How would you cope if a patch of sand turned out to be a cunningly disguised but deadly poisonous snake? It's going to be tough surviving in the desert, but don't despair! It might not seem possible as you gaze across the empty wastes, but people, animals and plants have lived in the desert for thousands of years. They'll be able to teach you a thing or two. All you need to do is read on...

WARNING! WANDERING ALONE IN THE DESERT CAN DAMAGE YOUR HEALTH. DON'T TRY THE SURVIVAL TIPS IN THIS BOOK WITHOUT A DESERT GUIDE TO HELP YOU.

If you closed your eyes and tried to imagine a desert, what would it be like? It would probably be a vast, open, sandy space, with rolling dunes and an oasis fringed with palm trees. There'd most likely be a camel or two appearing over the horizon. Some deserts are like this, but not all of them. In fact, the word 'desert' comes from a Latin word meaning any deserted place. The different types of desert are shown below.

WHAT IS A DESERT?

Some of the world's biggest deserts do live up to our expectations of what a typical desert should look like. They are very hot and very sandy. In a hot desert, such as the Sahara, the days are scorching hot but the nights can be close to freezing point. This is the pattern year in year out. But not all deserts are hot. In a cold desert, such as the Gobi, summers are warm and winters are freezing cold. All deserts have one thing in common, though - they are all very, very dry.

Tropical deserts
Tropical deserts occur on either side of the Equator in areas of high pressure where hot, dry air stops rainclouds from forming.

High pressure

Cold current

Coastal deserts
Coastal deserts are found in places where winds blow in off the sea, having been cooled by ocean currents. These winds carry very little moisture with them.

Rain-shadow deserts
These deserts lie on the sheltered side of mountains. By the time the wind reaches them, it has lost all its rain on the other side of the hills.

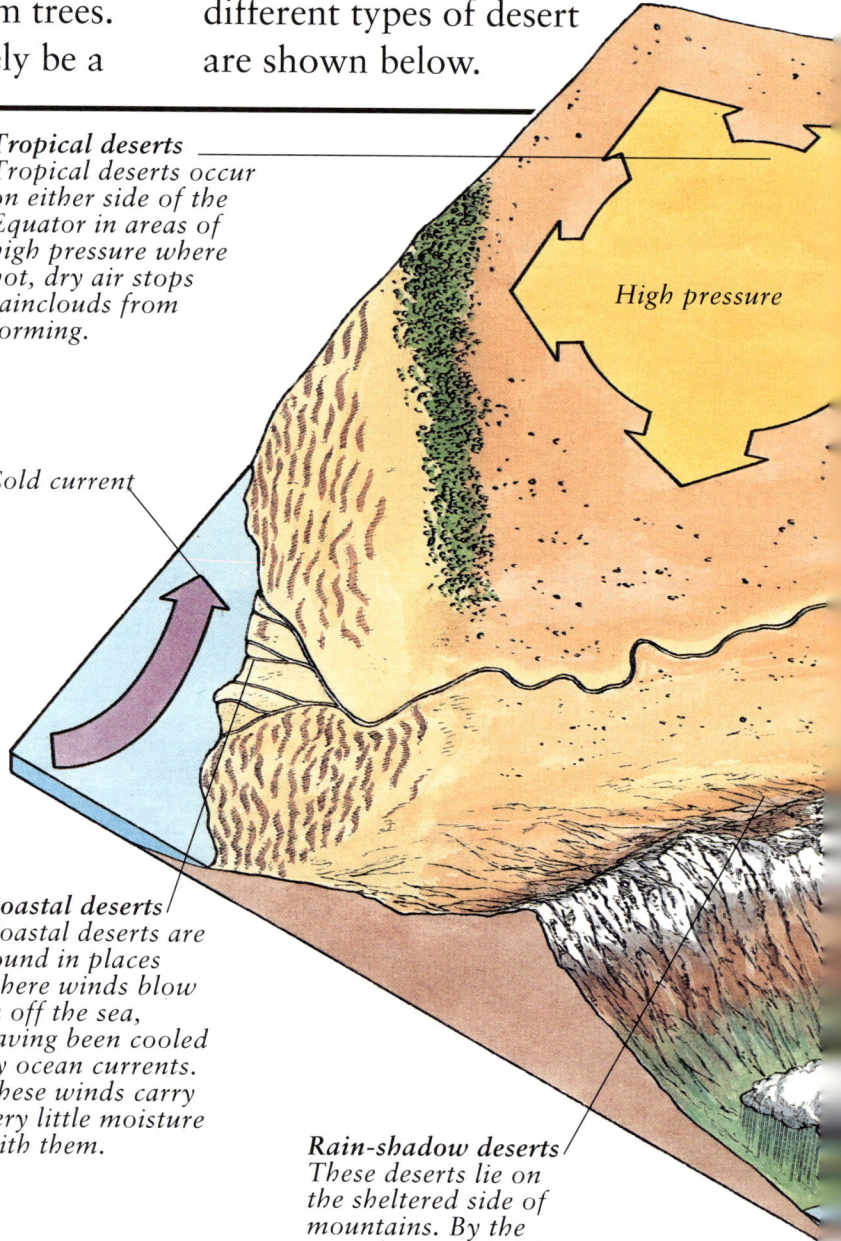

Inland deserts
Inland deserts are so far from the coast that winds blowing in off the sea have no moisture left by the time they reach them.

DESERT SPOTTING

Deserts may look barren and bare but they are home to a surprising number of animals and plants. You can use these to work out which desert you're in. If the camels have one hump, you may be in Arabia or Africa. If they have two, you're in the Gobi Desert. The American deserts have cacti!

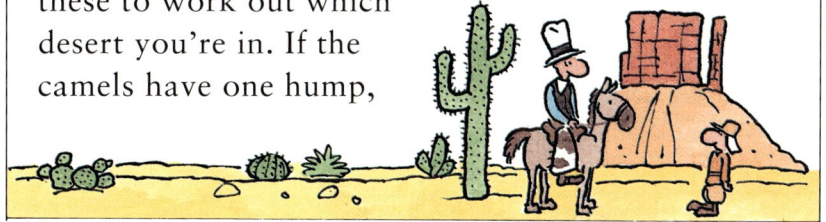

Dry air

Rainfall

DESERT LANDSCAPES
Sand is the most famous desert feature but it only covers about a quarter of all the world's deserts. Some deserts are gravelly, some are rocky; others are salty or made of ancient volcanic rock. Most are a mixture of sand and stones. In Arabic, sandy desert is called erg, stony desert is reg, rocky desert is called hammada.

Reg

Hammada

Salt flats

Rocky volcanic

Erg

Deserts cover over a fifth of the Earth. There are deserts in Africa, Asia, Australia, North and South America, and the Middle East. In fact, you'll find deserts in every continent, except Europe. Strictly speaking, even the icy wastes of Antarctica count as desert. As you've seen, deserts occur near the coast, far inland and in two areas of high pressure to the north and south of the Equator. These areas are called the horse latitudes.

DESERTS OF THE WORLD

The map on the right shows you the world's deserts, big and small. Where do you think you've ended up? Find out as much as you can about the area - any knowledge will help you to survive. The hot Sahara Desert in Africa is the largest desert, by far. About the size of the whole of the USA, it covers a third of Africa ... and it's getting bigger.

1 Great Basin
2 Death Valley
3 Mojave
4 Sonoran
5 Chihuahuan
6 Nacza
7 Atacama
8 Patagonian
9 Sahara
10 Nubian
11 Danakil
12 Namib
13 Kalahari
14 Arabian (includes Great Nafud; Nedjed; Rub 'al Khali; Hadhramaut; Hejaz)
15 Negev
16 Iranian (includes Dasht-e Kavir; Dasht-e Lut)
17 Turkestan (includes Kara Kum; Kyzyl Kum)
18 Thar
19 Takla Maka
20 Gobi
21 Great Sandy
22 Gibson
23 Simpson
24 Great Victoria
25 Sturt

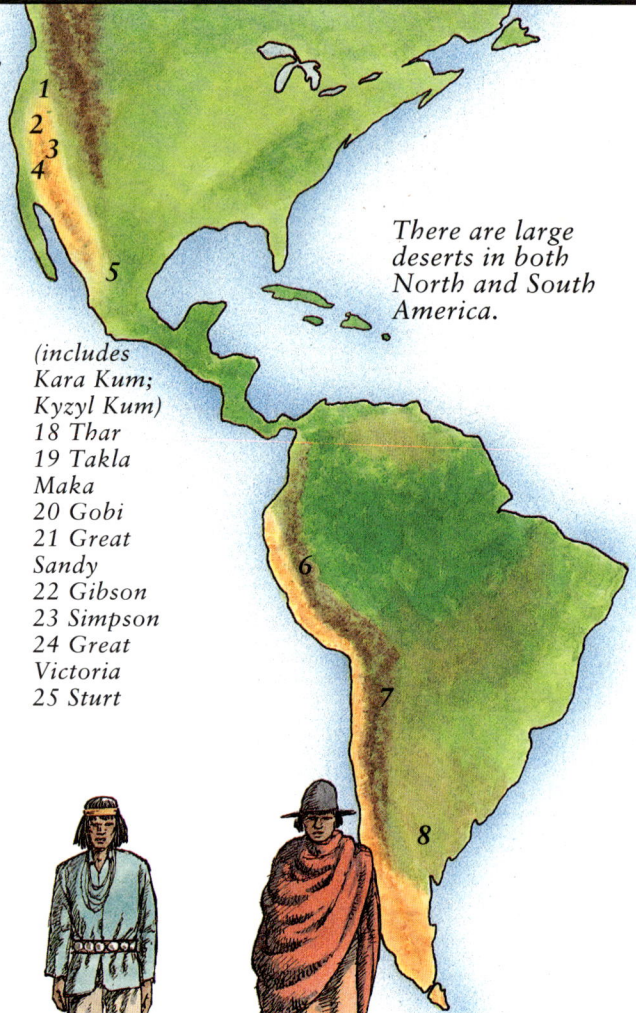

There are large deserts in both North and South America.

PEOPLE OF THE DESERT

Desert life is very hard, but some people have learnt to cope with the harsh conditions. Most desert dwellers are nomads. They wander from place to place in search of water and food. Some are herders, keeping camels, sheep and goats. Others hunt desert animals and gather plants and grubs to eat. There are thought to be about five million Bedouin, 110,000 Aborigines and 60,000 Bushmen living in the deserts.

Navajo
North American
deserts

South American
Indian
Atacama Desert

GROWING DESERTS

Many of the world's wild places are shrinking, but not the deserts. Most deserts are growing. People overuse the land at the edge of the desert. They cut down too many trees and graze too many animals until it, too, turns to desert.

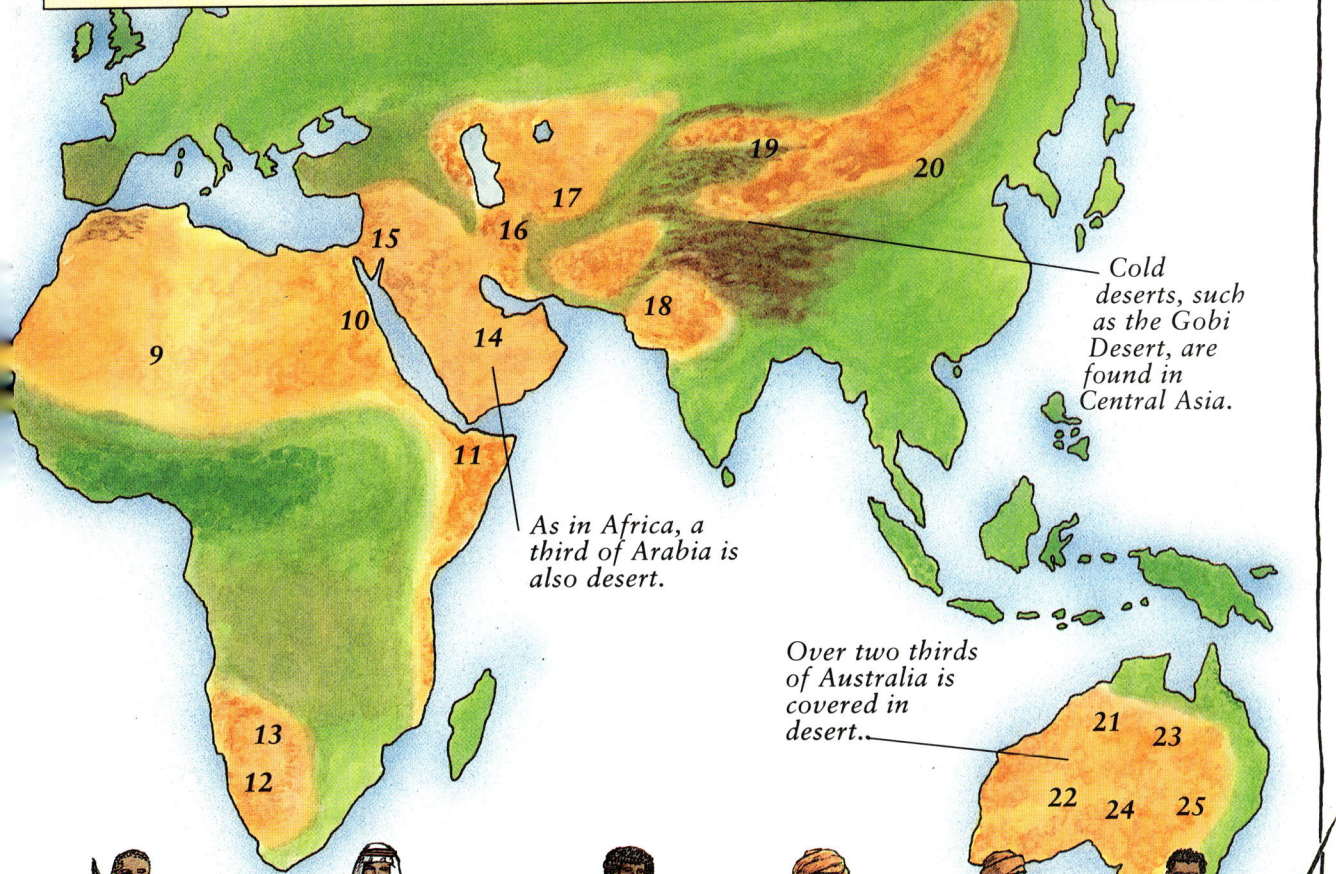

Cold deserts, such as the Gobi Desert, are found in Central Asia.

As in Africa, a third of Arabia is also desert.

Over two thirds of Australia is covered in desert.

15
17
19
20
16
18
10
14
9
11
13
12
21 23
22 24 25

Bushman Kalahari Desert

Bedouin Arabian Desert

Afar Danakil Desert

Rajasthani Thar Desert

Mongol Gobi Desert

Aborigine Australian deserts

Deserts are the driest places on Earth; some are the hottest places on Earth. So, how are you going to find enough water and stay cool enough to survive? The desert climate affects how people live, what they wear, eat and avoid. Desert people have been coping with these problems for thousands of years. Now it's your turn! But first you need to know a bit more about the weather in the desert, and about the weird and wonderful effects it has.

DESERT WEATHER

Deserts are places which have less than 25cm of rain a year. Months or years may go by without any rain. Then it may fall all at once, in a mighty downpour. Dried-up river beds, or wadis, fill to overflowing and there are flash floods. Clouds are very rare in the desert. This is why there is so little rain.

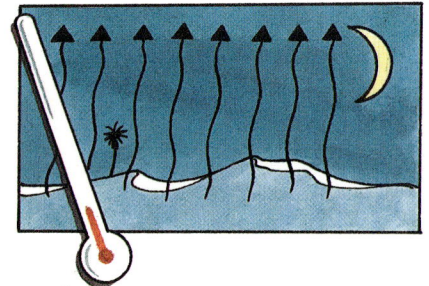

DAYTIME AND NIGHTTIME

The lack of rainclouds means that hot deserts are scorching in the day because there is no shade, but can be bitterly cold at night because there are no clouds to trap the heat. In the Sahara, the temperature can reach 55°C in the day but plummet below freezing at night.

Arch

Mushroom rock

Parallel dunes

Barchan dunes

Seif dunes

Star dunes

Inselberg

Sand dunes have different shapes, depending on how the wind blows. Dunes in the Sahara can rise over 400m high. They move and bury villages and oases.

Wind-blown sand eats away at layers of soft rock, carving them into strange shapes. It also smooths and shines the surface of pebbles.

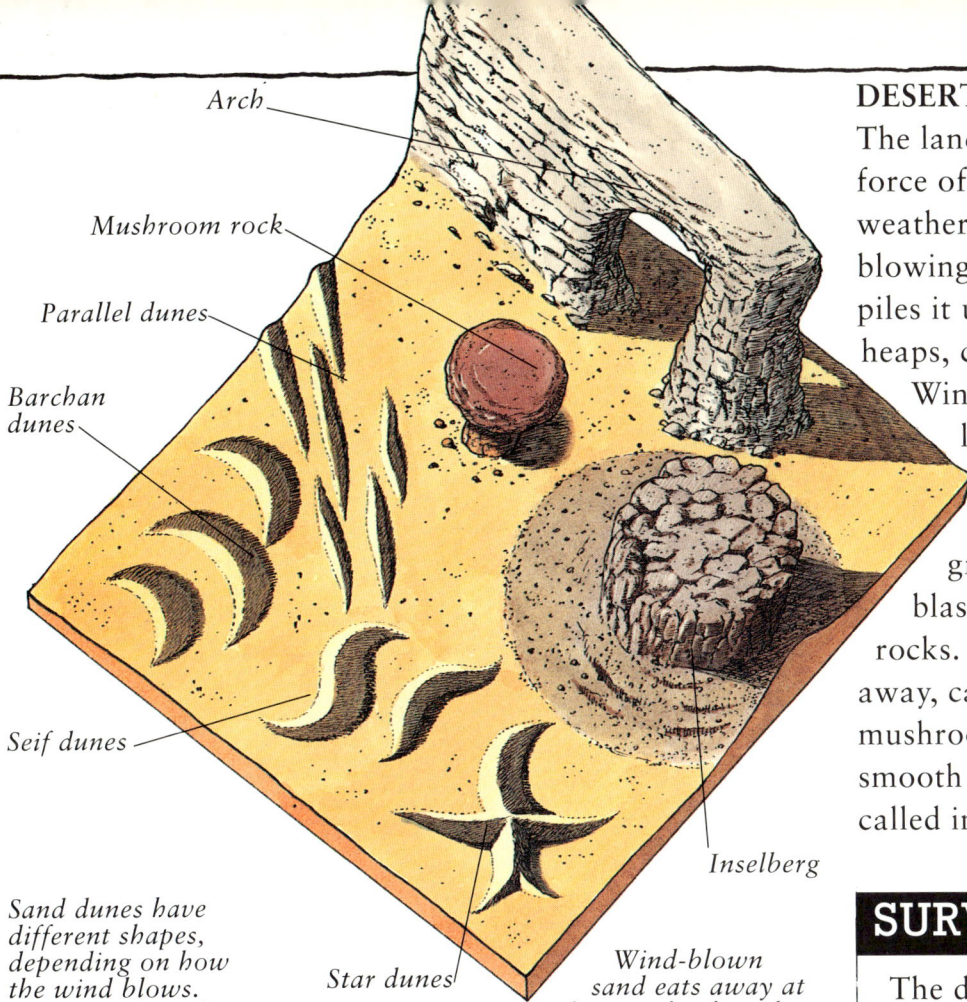

DESERT SCULPTURES

The land feels the full force of the desert weather, too. Wind blowing over the sand piles it up into huge heaps, called sand dunes. Wind-blown sand acts like a giant pad of sandpaper. The wind picks up the grains of sand and blasts them at the rocks. They eat the rocks away, carving out arches, mushrooms and great smooth slabs of rocks, called inselbergs.

SURVIVAL TIP 1

The desert weather can play funny tricks on people so don't be fooled by the sight of an oasis on the horizon. It may be a mirage, caused by the hot desert air distorting the light from a far-distant oasis.

DUST STORMS

If the sky gets darker and the wind starts up, watch out! A dust storm is on its way. Cover your nose and mouth with a damp hanky to keep the choking dust out.

SAND STORMS

Sand storms are another desert hazard. Cover up well - sand stings! It is blasted along with such force it can strip the paint from a car.

SOLD OUT

COPING WITH THE HEAT

The desert can get very, very hot indeed and one of the desert dwellers' top priorities is to protect themselves from the Sun, and from the sand. Bedouin and Tuareg nomads wear long, loose, flowing robes which let cool air circulate inside. They also cover their heads and faces. Your best bet is to model your desert gear on theirs. Choose light-coloured cotton clothes - they'll keep you cooler.

EXPLORER FACTS

In 1828, René Caillié became the first European explorer to reach Timbuktu and return alive - across the Sahara. He had spent three years learning how to live and speak Arabic as local people did - the secret of his success.

Head and neck protected from sunburn and heatstroke.

Cloth wrapped round face to keep the sand out.

Loose robes protect the whole body from sunburn and keep it cool.

Camels store fat in their humps, for food.

Skinks burrow into the sand to escape the heat and their enemies.

Camels have wide, splayed feet which stop them sinking in the soft sand.

Many plants have thick, waxy leaves to cut down water loss and prevent them drying out in the Sun.

Camels have double eyelashes to keep the sand out of their eyes.

A camel can close its nostrils against the sand.

The glare from the desert Sun is strong so wear sunglasses to protect your eyes. If you don't have any, cut two slits in some card or bark and use this instead. Smearing soot under your eyes also helps.

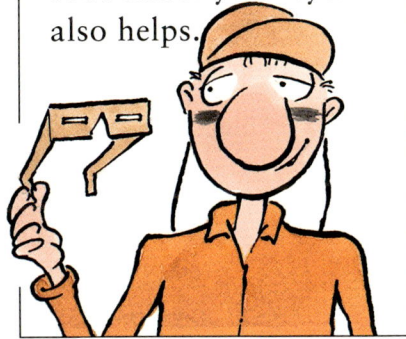

HIDING FROM THE HEAT

Desert animals have various ways of coping with the heat and dust. Camels are perfectly adapted to desert life. Apart from the special features shown here, they can also go for a month without water. Many small animals are nocturnal. They spend the day underground, where it can be 30°C cooler than on the surface. Others shelter inside cacti, under rocks or in the shade of their own tails. If desert tortoises get too hot, they wet their heads and necks with cooling saliva.

A hat is essential.

Sunglasses

Scarf to cover face

Neck protection

Cover up well in baggy, cotton clothes.

Water bottle and as much water as you can carry

Bag for extra clothes for the night, and for suncream

Sturdy footwear Never go barefoot - you'll burn your feet.

Compass

The ground is much hotter than the air above it. Camels and ostriches are tall enough to reach the cooler air.

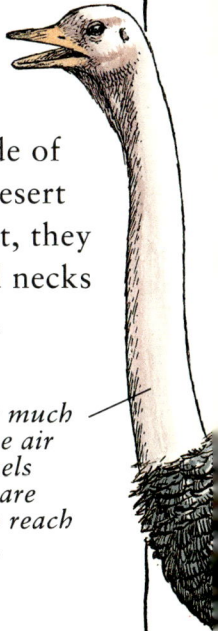

Most desert insects spend the day underground in the shade.

The Kalahari squirrel uses its bushy tail as a sunshade.

Jerboas and gerbils shelter from the heat of the day in cool underground burrows.

Snakes and tortoises shelter by shady bushes or rocks. Their scales and shells also protect them from the Sun.

SHELTER IN THE DESERT

Like everything else in the desert, homes and shelters are affected by the weather. People can't burrow underground like the animals on the previous page, but they do need somewhere shady to shelter from the fierce Sun. Nomadic people also need homes which fit in with their wandering lifestyles. Their homes need to be light and easy to carry from place to place. What could be better for people on the move than a tent?

Yurts
Winter can be very cold in the Gobi Desert. Mongol nomads live in circular tents, called yurts, made of wood lined with felt for warmth.

NOMADS

Bedouin tents have flaps at the sides which can be raised to let a breeze circulate during the day and lowered to keep the warmth in at night. Inside, a curtain divides the men's and women's areas.

Black or white tents
In some areas, Bedouin tribes make 'black' tents of dark goat hair. Other tribes make 'white' tents of sheep's wool and white goat hair.

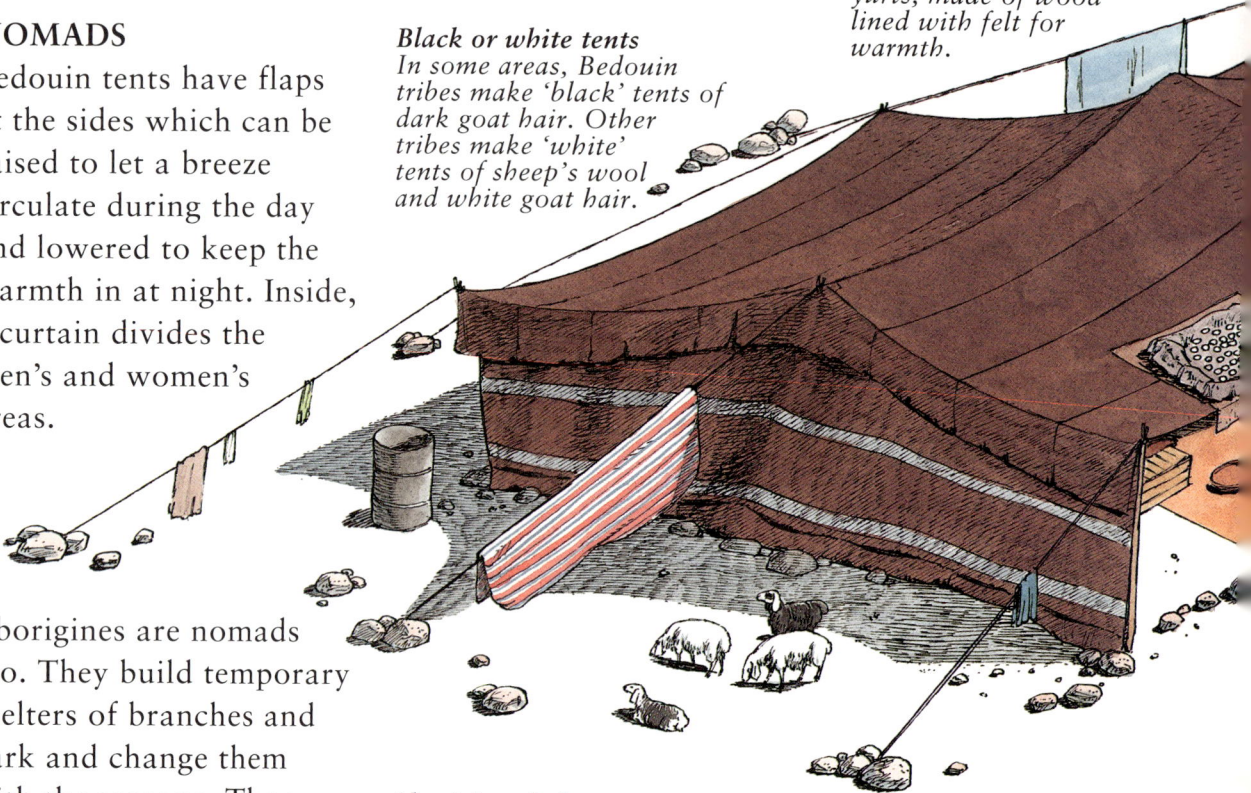

Aborigines are nomads too. They build temporary shelters of branches and bark and change them with the seasons. There are bark tents for the chilly winter, thatched, round huts for the worst of the rainy season, and raised sleeping platforms with fires underneath for times when mosquitoes are about.

Aborigine shelters

Round huts made from grass and bark

Tent-like hut made from bark

Anti-mosquito platform, raised on poles

12

Houses of hair
The Bedouin make their tents, or 'houses of hair', from camel, goat or sheep hair woven into long strips which are sewn together. Inside the tent, they sit and sleep on woven carpets.

When the Bedouin move camp, the tents are taken down, rolled up and packed on to the backs of camels.

SETTLERS

There are some permanent settlements and towns in the desert. They have usually grown up around oases where there is plenty of water for keeping animals and for growing crops, such as dates. Some of the bigger towns have markets where nomads from the surrounding desert can come to buy and sell goods.

Oasis town in Morocco

Hopi pueblo, USA

Navajo homes in Arizona, USA

Mens' area
The men sit apart, on the other side of the curtain. They have a small fire over which they make coffee. They also keep the camel saddles here.

Women's area
Cooking utensils, chests of clothes, bedding and sacks of dates and grain are kept in the women's area.

The women weave the hair for the tents into strips and sew them into larger panels. Most tents are about 12m long and five metres wide.

SURVIVAL TIP 3

Nighttime in the desert can be bitterly cold. Choose carefully where to rest. First find a rock to lie against and make your fire in front of it. Build a pile of rocks opposite the fire to maximise its heat, by reflection.

EATING WITHOUT BEING EATEN

Food takes second place to water in the desert, but you still need to keep your strength up and not go hungry. Looking around, food may seem to be hard to find... But local people manage to find enough to eat. They hunt animals, gather roots, tubers and insects, herd animals and even farm in places where there is enough water. Years of experience have also taught them which animals and plants to avoid.

HUNTING FOR FOOD

If you were an Aborigine or a Bushman you would find food for your family by hunting and gathering. Only the men of the tribe go hunting. Young boys are taught to hunt by their fathers. The hunters track their prey, often for many days, before they make a kill. They use a variety of weapons - bows and poison-tipped arrows for the Bushmen, boomerangs, spears and even guns for the Aborigines. They also use hunting dogs which chase after prey and help to bring it down.

Among the Navajo Indian tribes in the deserts of North America, it is the women who go out hunting on horseback.

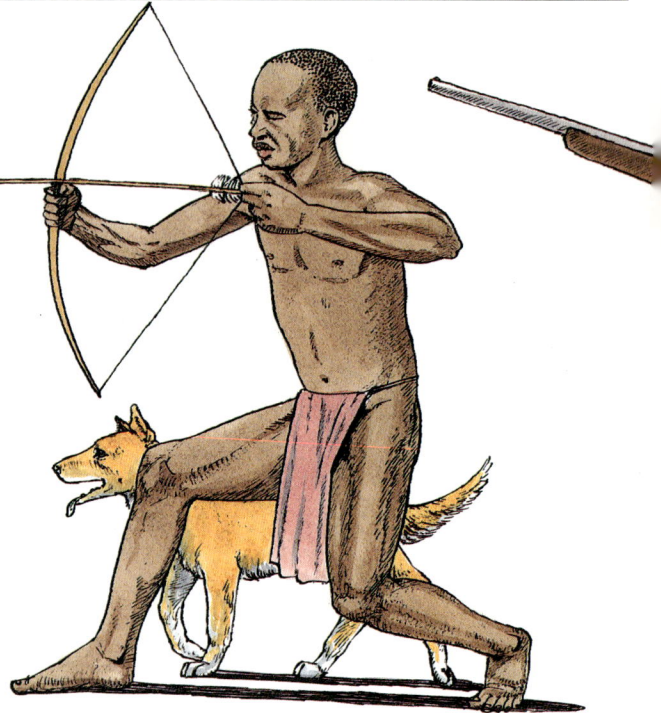

Below you can see some of the animals which might appear on a Bushman menu. A hunter gains great respect if he kills a large animal, such as an antelope.

Guinea fowl   Sandgrouse   Spring hare   Ostrich   Antelope   Scrub hare   Porcupine

The flat, curved boomerang is the Aborigines' most famous weapon. It is used for bringing down prey such as kangaroos and emus.

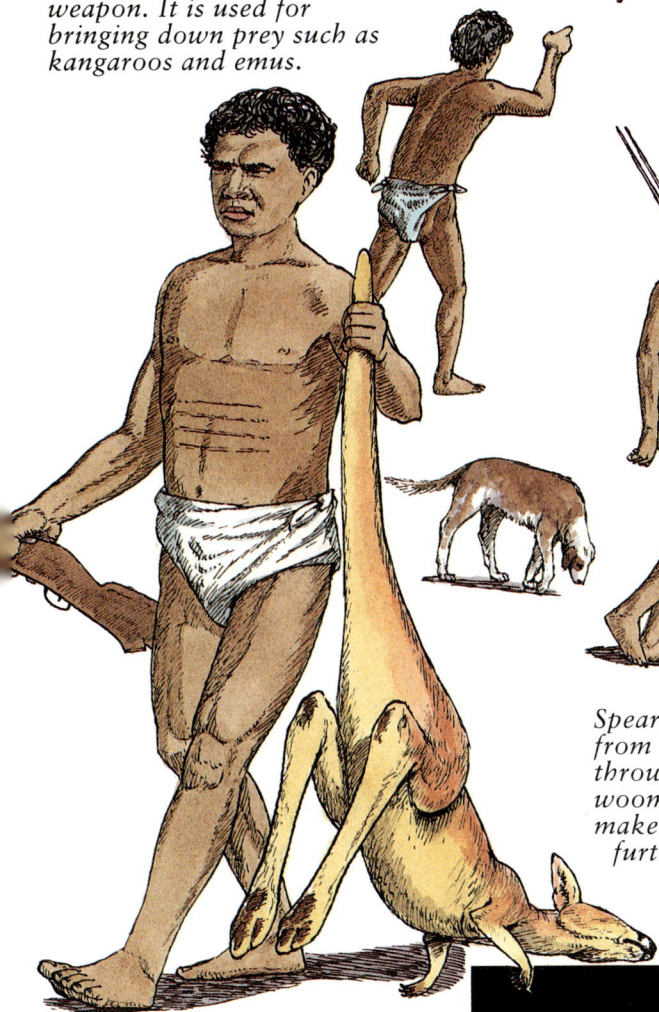

Honeypot ants

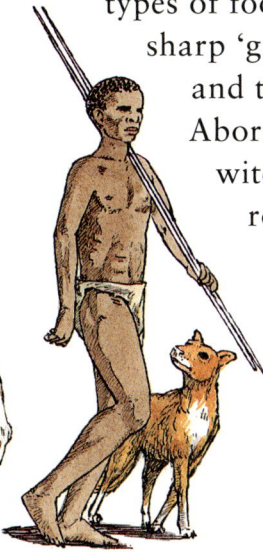

GATHERING FOOD

While the men go off hunting, the women and children search for other types of food. They use sharp 'grubbing' sticks to dig roots and tubers out of the ground. Aborigines collect nutty-tasting witchetty grubs which they eat roasted. They also know where to find honeypot ants, whose bodies are bloated with honey. These make tasty sweets. The Bushmen collect mungongo nuts from the desert trees.

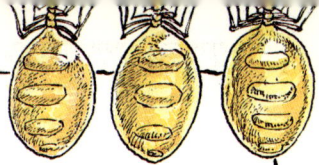

Cracking open mungongo nuts

Spears are launched from wooden spear throwers, called woomeras. They make the spear go further and faster.

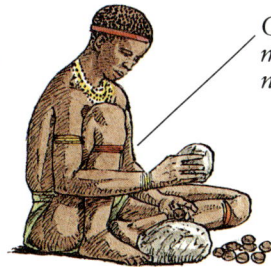

How do you fancy eating charcoaled kangaroo steak or juicy roast goanna (monitor lizard) like the Aborigines do?

Wallaby Kangaroo Goanna

EXPLORER FACTS

Flinders River

Cooper's Creek

Sydney

Melbourne

Starvation caused the deaths of the explorers, Burke and Wills, on the return part of their epic journey across Australia in 1860. They reached their supply camp at Cooper's Creek, only to find that it had been abandoned just seven hours earlier. Burke and Wills died by the side of the Creek.

Burke and Wills

NOMAD HERDERS

Some desert people, such as the Bedouin, Tuareg and Mongols, are nomads but they rely on their herds of camels, sheep and goats for meat, milk, wool and leather. They move from place to place in search of better grazing and water for their animals. In the hottest, driest parts of the year, they pitch camp near an oasis or a well.

Date palm

PRECIOUS LIVESTOCK

Camels are the most important animals kept by the desert herdsmen. They are used for food, transport and as a sign of wealth and prestige. Camels are traded for other goods, given as gifts and used to pay fines. To stop them wandering away from the camp at night, their front legs are tied together, or hobbled. Watchdogs guard the camp, and the camels!

Llamas
Llamas take the place of camels (their close relations) in the deserts of South America. They provide meat, milk and transport.

One hump or two
Arabian camels, or dromedaries, have one hump only. Two-humped camels come from Central Asia. They are called Bactrian camels.

Hobbling

Camel cart
Camels are immensely strong and can carry heavy loads. Bactrian camels are often used to pull carts full of a family's belongings.

SHEEP AND GOATS

Flocks of sheep and goats are kept for their milk and wool. A sheep may be killed for a special feast.

DESERT FARMING

Some Bedouin nomads farm small patches of desert, growing wheat and barley and harvesting dates. As soon as it rains, scouts are sent out from the camp to find a good area to farm. Word is sent to the camp and the men come to plough and sow. Camels are used to plough.

SALTY MILK AND BUTTER

Camel, sheep and goat milk is salted to stop it going sour or it is made into butter or cheese. Sheep's butter is made by putting the milk in a goatskin bag and churning it for a couple of hours.

Goatskin butter churn

CAMEL-BACK HUNTING

Wealthy Bedouin chiefs sometimes go gazelle or hyena hunting on camel-back with their speedy salukis (dogs like greyhounds) and falcons. Children also get the salukis to chase jerboas which they roast and share with their dogs!

Wandering from place to place is all very well but it can be very tiring and energy-sapping if you're not used to it. Make sure you drink some salt dissolved in water to replace the salt you lose when you sweat.

MARKET TIME

Traders from nearby towns and villages visit the Bedouin camps to buy and sell things. The nomads also make trips to the market to exchange camels for fruit, cloth, saddles and other equipment.

ESSENTIAL WATER

As you'll know by now, surviving in the desert is thirsty work. Human beings need nine litres of water a day to live. Without water you'd be dead in two days. And you can lose a litre of water in an hour just by sweating. But don't get downhearted! There is water in the desert - it's just a case of knowing where to look for it. An oasis is an obvious start. Here water from underground creates a rare fertile patch of land. But local people are the best source of information about finding water. Plants and animals have ingenious ways of finding and storing water too.

Oasis

Qanats
Qanats are underground, man-made tunnels which bring water from a distant source. Wells are sunk down into them to draw up the water for irrigation.

Irrigation
A shaduf is a device used in Egypt for raising water from the River Nile to irrigate fields so that crops can be grown.

EXPLORER FACTS

Francis Younghusband, an officer in the British army, crossed the Gobi Desert in 1886. With him he took a large supply of sherry to quench his thirst in case he ran out of water!

BLOOMING DESERTS

After a rare shower of rain, the desert may suddenly burst into bloom. Ephemeral plants have seeds which lie underground for months or even years until it is wet enough to flower.

SURVIVAL TIP 5

In an emergency, you can collect water using a solar still. Dig a hole in the sand and put a cup in the centre of the hole. Cover the hole with a plastic sheet, weighted down with rocks. Water vapour from the soil will condense on to the plastic and fall into the cup.

RICH RIVER NILE

Irrigation has made the land along the River Nile rich and fertile. Beyond it is dusty desert.

Sandgrouse

Desert vine

Bitter apple

Why not quench your thirst with a frog!

Darkling beetle

—*Baobab tree*

FINDING WATER

Bushmen suck up underground water through hollow reeds and store it in empty ostrich eggshells. Aborigines sometimes squeeze a drink from a frog which stores water in its body! Many plants store water too.

Bushmen collect underground water from 'sipwells'.

ANIMALS AND WATER

Jerboas don't need to drink. They get all the water they need from seeds they eat. The darkling beetle of the Namib Desert collects droplets of sea fog on its body. Sandgrouse soak their breast feathers in water and their chicks suck it off.

Jerboa

DANGER IN THE DESERT

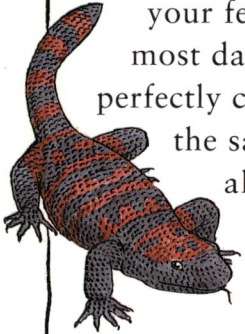

You need to watch where you're putting your feet in the desert. Some of the most dangerous desert creatures are perfectly camouflaged to blend in with the sand! But don't be too alarmed. Although dangerous animals do lurk, they won't bother you if you leave them well alone. Local people never tease or torment *Gila monster* these creatures and neither should you. If you do disturb an animal accidentally, move quickly and quietly out of its way.

EXPLORER FACTS

The explorer, David Livingstone, crossed the Kalahari Desert in 1851. On his travels, he ran out of water and food, and was attacked and nearly killed by a lion.

All these animals come from different deserts.

Dingoes and wild dogs
Dingoes and hyenas are wild dogs. They can be quite vicious and may steal any food you leave lying around your camp.

Mountain lion
Mountain lions or pumas live in the North American deserts. They are considered sacred by desert Indians.

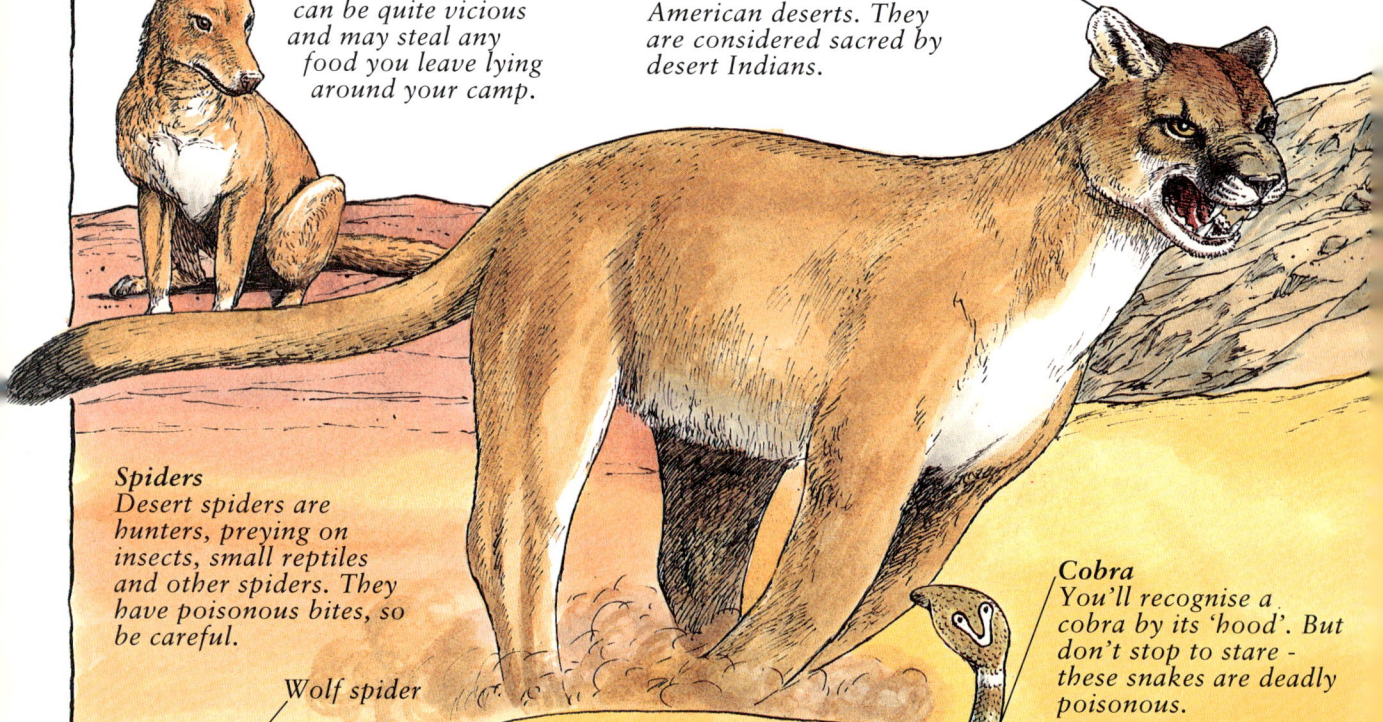

Spiders
Desert spiders are hunters, preying on insects, small reptiles and other spiders. They have poisonous bites, so be careful.

Cobra
You'll recognise a cobra by its 'hood'. But don't stop to stare - these snakes are deadly poisonous.

Wolf spider

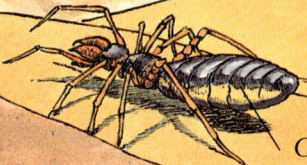

Camel spider

20

Coyote
Another wild dog is the coyote of North America, a survivor, despite years of being hunted.

Always shake out your boots in case a snake or scorpion is snoozing in them. If you are bitten by a snake, you'll need medical help. Keep still so the poison doesn't spread.

Spider-hunting wasps
Some wasps paralyse spiders and lay eggs on them. The wasp grubs then have a ready meal when they hatch.

Shake, rattle and roll
If you hear an eerie rattling, keep well away. This is the warning sound made by a deadly poisonous rattlesnake before it strikes.

Sidewinder tracks
Sidewinder snakes leave tell-tale S-shaped tracks on the ground. Look out for these as you walk along.

EXPLORER FACTS

In 1876, the German explorer, Erwin von Barry, claimed he'd seen crocodile tracks in the Sahara Desert. Nobody believed him until 30 years later when a crocodile was shot in the Sahara.

Scorpion
Scorpions have very nasty stings in the tips of their tails. First they arch their tails over, then they sting.

Horned viper
All you may see of the highly poisonous horned viper is its two horns poking out of the sand.

Local people are the key to your survival in the desert. Their knowledge will be invaluable. In return, be careful to respect their way of life. Desert people have their own religions and beliefs, customs and languages. They are also famous for their hospitality. Be sure to respond politely if your host offers you the sheep's eyeball. It is reserved especially for honoured guests.

ARAB RELIGION

Like many Arab people, the Bedouin are Muslims as are the Tuareg. Their religion is Islamic. Muslims believe in Allah (God) and in his most important prophet, Muhammad.

In their daily life, they follow a set of rules called the five pillars of Islam. By obeying these, they believe they will go to heaven. Muslims worship in mosques. Wherever they are, they always face Mecca when they pray. Strict Muslims pray five times a day. Mecca is a city in the desert of Saudi Arabia. It is the Muslims' holiest place. They try to make a pilgrimage to Mecca, called the Haj, at least once in their lives.

Desert mosque

Mecca

EXPLORER FACTS

Ibn Battuta (1304-1378) was the greatest Muslim explorer. A journey to Mecca in 1325 gave him a taste for travelling. In total, he travelled over 120,000km.

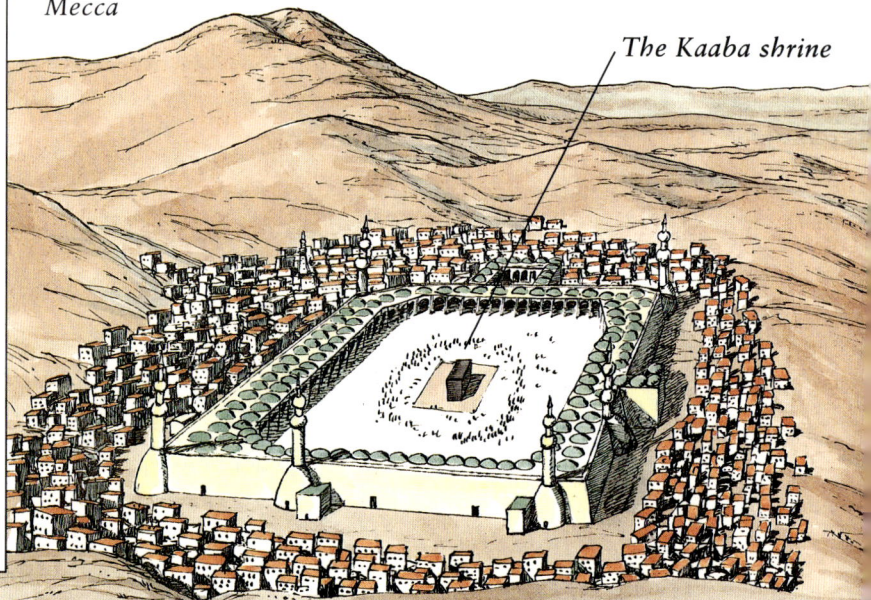

The Kaaba shrine

SACRED PAINTINGS

Many Aboriginal paintings show scenes taken from Dreamtime. They are often painted on rocks and cave walls. Other sacred paintings have been found in the Nacza Desert in Peru. Huge birds and animals have been carved into the rock, some 2,500 years ago. They include a pelican and a condor.

Aboriginal rock painting

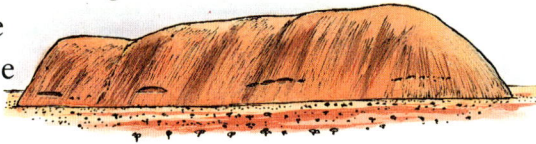

DREAMTIME

The Aborigine religion is made up of hundreds of myths and beliefs about the world around them. It is closely linked with their home and its well-being. Many rocks are considered to be sacred, including Ayers Rock. They are thought to be the homes of the spirits. The Aborigines believe that the land as it is today was created in a period called Dreamtime. Before this, the world was a flat, grey place. Giant mythical creatures roamed the land, creating its features and the plants and animals.

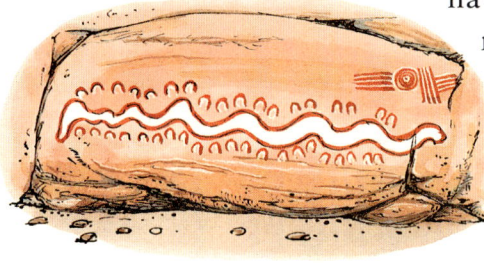

Ayers Rock

Pelican, Nacza Desert

MAGICAL POWERS

Magic plays a big part in the everyday lives and beliefs of many desert people. This witchdoctor (shaman) is looking at jackal tracks left in a magic square in the sand. Aborigines use magic to help them hunt, to bring rain and to treat any members of the tribe who become ill.

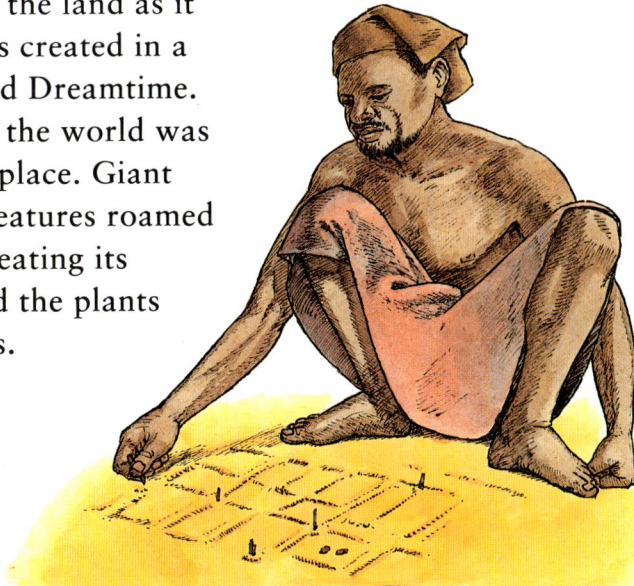

WEAVING

Traditionally, all Bedouin women learn how to weave using hair and wool from their camels, goats and sheep. They make strips for the tents, dividing curtains, carpets and rugs for sitting and praying on, saddle bags for the camels and so on. The cloth for the tents is usually kept plain brown, black or white, but for other things it is dyed blue, red, yellow and green.

Tribal patterns
Each tribe has its own characteristic pattern of triangles, zig-zags and diamonds which is worked into the weaving. They use different patterns of colours, too.

Loom
The women use simple wooden looms, laid out on the ground. They work at one end, in the shade.

SURVIVAL TIP 7

If you're staying with a Bushman or Aborigine, be careful what you do with your hands! You might be saying something you shouldn't. Hunters use hand signals so that they can communicate with each other silently. If they shouted and screamed, they'd soon scare the animals off. Many of the signals show features of an animal, such as horns.

Bushman hand signals
Hawk   Duck   Scrub hare   Lion   **Aborigine signal**
Who are you?

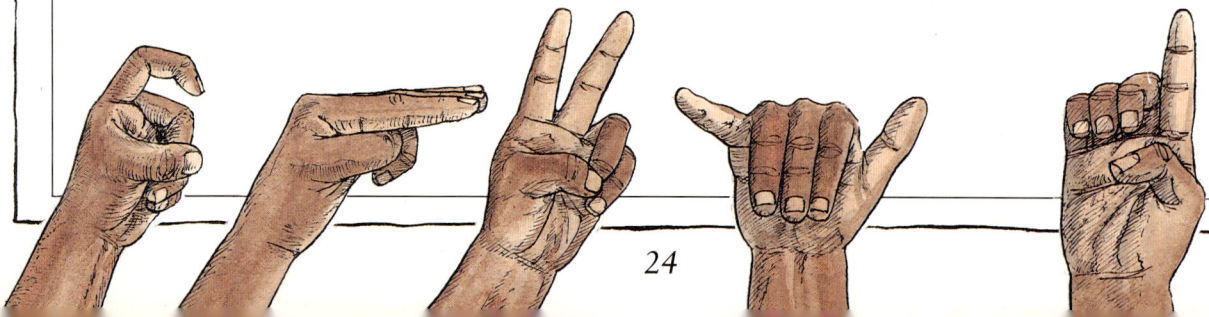

ABORIGINAL ART

The art and crafts of desert people are closely linked to their religion or beliefs and to the animals and plants around them. Aborgine artists often paint pictures of animals on pieces of eucalyptus bark, using paints made from clay or charcoal mixed with water.

SCARS AND TATTOOES

Aborigines paint their bodies in preparation for dancing (see next page). Boys also have cuts made in their chests. The scars show that they are now grown up. Bedouin woman have their hands and faces tattooed. This is thought to make them look more beautiful.

Aborigines with chest scars

Bedouin woman with hand and face tattooes

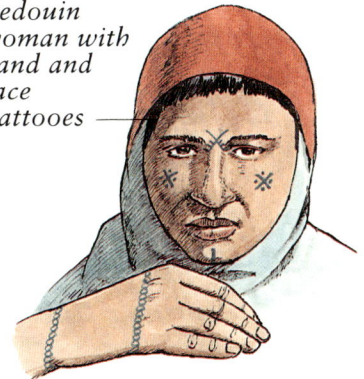

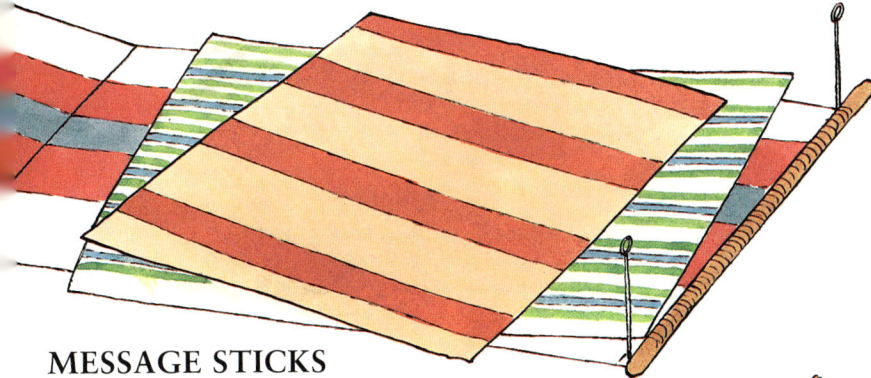

MESSAGE STICKS

Many Aborigine tribes use carved sticks to send messages. A stick might record an unpaid debt, or act as an invitation to a hunt, a funeral or some other tribal ceremony.

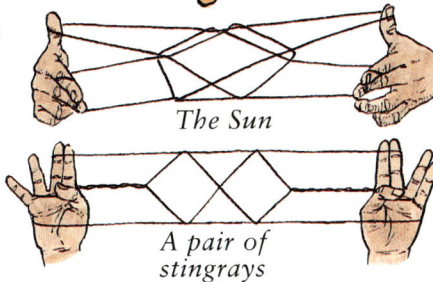

The Sun

A pair of stingrays

FUN AND GAMES

Finjan is a favourite Bedouin game. The players are divided into two teams. Team A hides a ring under one of 12 coffee cups. Team B has to guess which cup it's under.

CAT'S-CRADLE

Aborigines do cat's-cradle with strings of bark fibre. They tell stories by weaving the string into figures.

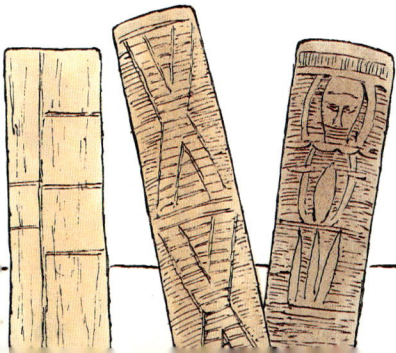

HAVING A FEAST DAY

In Bedouin tribes, special occasions such as weddings are the cause of great celebrations. The bridegroom's father acts as the host. Sheep or camels are slaughtered for the feast. The wedding celebrations last for a week.

The bridegroom's father had to give the bride's father a number of camels as a wedding dowry.

The men sit and eat apart from the women. The bridegroom serves them with coffee.

The bride is dressed in special clothes and jewellery. She travels to the wedding tent by camel.

STAYING FOR COFFEE

The Bedouin are very hospitable. They will always offer guests food and a place to stay. The first and most important part of welcoming a guest is the coffee-making ceremony. The coffee beans are roasted over the fire, then ground with a pestle and mortar. Then it is brewed with boiling water and served. Coffee is drunk strong, black and very sweet. By drinking it, you accept the tribe's hospitality.

Making coffee

Serving coffee

SURVIVAL TIP 8

In many Muslim countries, women keep their heads covered as a sign of modesty. The Bedouin would not take kindly to you turning up in shorts or your swim—suit. They'll make you very welcome if you respect their ways.

Rebaba

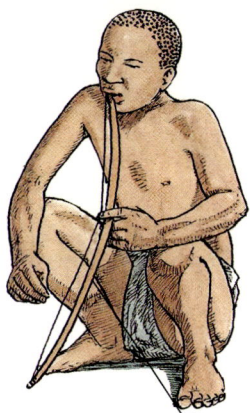

Musical bow

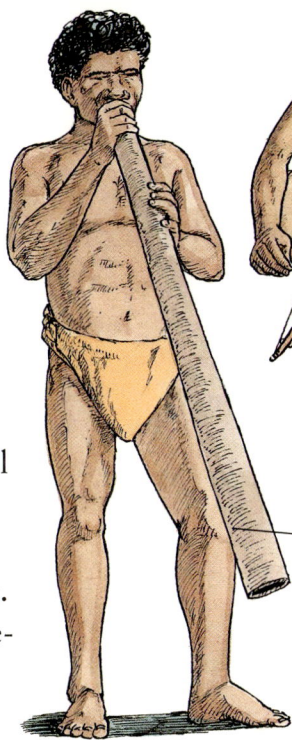

Didgeridoo

INITIATION RITES

An Aborigine boy has to undergo trials of strength and bravery to be counted as an adult. They may include fire-walking and being covered in sacred blood.

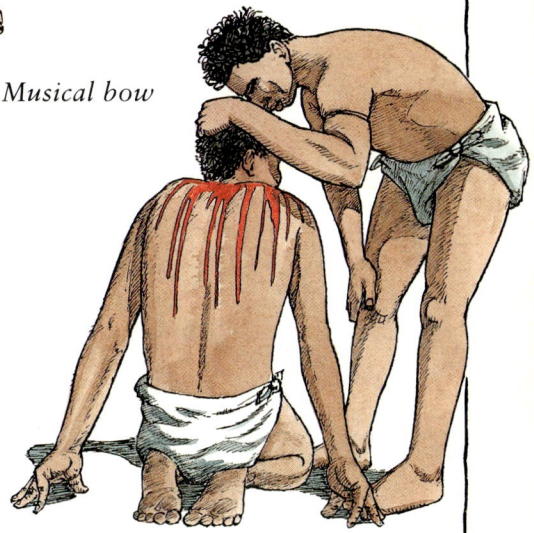

MUSIC TIME

Desert people have various types of musical instruments to accompany dancing, singing and storytelling. The Bedouin play a one-stringed fiddle, called a rebaba. Bushmen pluck bows which have been adapted from their hunting bows. Aborigines blow down long, wooden didgeridoos.

DANCING AND TRANCING

Aborigines have dances for all occasions - weddings, funerals and before they go hunting. They also have many ancient ritual dances which act out important myths. The steps for these dances are handed down from father to son.

Whilst in a trance, a Bushman may pick up or walk over hot coals without getting burnt.

Before a kangaroo hunt, the men imitate the actions of kangaroos in their dancing.

The Bushmen dance too. Some also fall into deep trances as they dance. A trance is thought to bestow magical powers on the person involved.

GETTING ABOUT AND OUT

You've had a great time in the Bedouin camp, drinking coffee and making new friends, but it's now time for you to find your way out of the desert. Easier said than done, you might say. It's not difficult to lose your bearings in the desert, where one stretch of sand and rock looks much like another. Don't give up! There are plenty of tips on these two pages to help you make your escape.

GETTING ABOUT

For centuries, the Bedouin and other desert herdsmen have used camels for transport. Some use Land Rovers, too. But the advantage of camels is that they don't get stuck in the sand. Some roads run through the desert in oil-rich countries such as Saudi Arabia. But the trusty camel is still the supreme 'ship of the desert', even though its swaying walk may make you feel slightly seasick.

EXPLORER FACTS

An English clergyman, Geoffrey Howard, crossed the Sahara in 1975, pushing a wheelbarrow full of supplies all the way!

EXPLORER FACTS

A monk, Hsuan Tsang (602-664), travelled from China to India to study Buddhism. His guides abandoned him in the Gobi Desert and he had to find his way by following trails of camel dung.

Bushmen and Aborigines travel by foot. It might seem aimless to us, but they know exactly where they are going when they wander in search of food. Young Aborigine men spend several years exploring the desert around them and learning survival skills. This period is called 'walkabout'.

For many of these desert tribespeople frontiers, or national borders, have no meaning as they wander along their ancient routes.

If you don't have a compass, you can use the Sun to help you get a sense of direction. In the northern hemisphere, point the hour hand of your watch at the Sun. True south is midway between the hour hand and the 12. In the southern hemisphere, point the 12 at the Sun and the mid point between the 12 and the hour hand is true north.

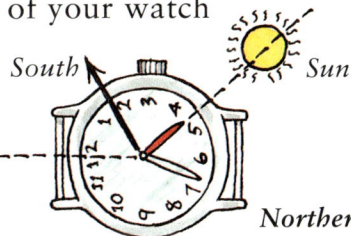

South *Sun*

Northern hemisphere

North *Sun*

Southern hemisphere

NAVIGATING BY THE STARS

If you're in the northern hemisphere, find the Big Dipper. To find the North Star, trace a straight line from the two stars in the end of the 'dip'. If you're in the southern hemisphere, look for the stars of the Southern Cross. The star at the foot of the cross points towards the south.

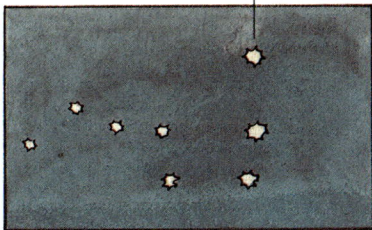

North Star

Big Dipper

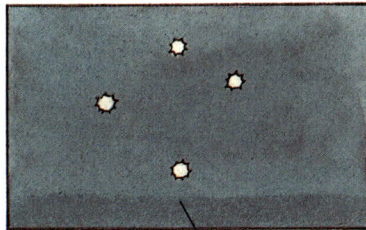

Southern Cross

To the south

SENDING SIGNALS

A good way of attracting attention is to find an open piece of ground and make a large sign or the word 'SOS' in rocks.

DESERT RICHES

While you're trying your hardest to get out of the desert, other people are trying to get in. They come in search of the huge amounts of precious mineral resources which have recently been discovered in the desert.

The most important of the desert's riches is oil. Enormous quantities of oil have been found under the desert in the Middle East, making some countries very wealthy. There are other minerals in the desert too - gold and opals in Australia, copper in Chile, diamonds in the Kalahari and silver in Mexico.

RECLAIMING THE DESERT

Next time you visit the desert, it may have changed. In some countries, people are trying to find ways of making better use of the deserts. After all, such huge, open spaces and such large amounts of sunshine shouldn't go to waste. So, some small parts of deserts are going green, with millions of litres of water being pumped into them so that crops can grow. But don't worry - there'll be lots of sand left!

THE GREEN DESERT

In North Africa, the Middle East and Israel, major irrigation schemes have turned some areas of desert into fertile fields. Water is diverted from rivers or collected from nearby hillsides. Computers are sometimes used to control the water supply. Farmers can now grow wheat, melons, avocados and even peaches in the fertile green fields which have been created in the desert.

In some countries in the Middle East, millions of litres of water are used to keep desert golf courses green!

The Negev Desert covers over half of the country of Israel.

Circular wheat fields in the Libyan desert are watered by rotating sprinklers.

SOLAR POWER

Solar power stations could be used to trap the energy of the desert Sun and convert it into electricity. A solar power station is already operating in the desert in California. Many more deserts could follow.

GLOSSARY

Adapted Suited to living in a particular place because of special physical features or lifestyle.

Desert The name given to the driest places on Earth. A desert gets less than 25cm of rain a year.

Didgeridoo An Aboriginal musical instrument, made from a long, wooden tube.

Ephemerals Plants which spring up after rain and quickly complete their life-cycle before dying away again. Their seeds can lie in the ground for many years, waiting for rain.

Erg Arabic word for sandy desert.

Hammada Arabic word for a desert covered in huge stretches of bare rock.

High pressure An area of high pressure is created where heavy, cold air sinks.

Horse latitudes Two bands of high pressure on either side of the Equator.

Inselberg A slab of rock which sticks up in the middle of the landscape. Its name means 'island mountain'.

Irrigation The regular supply of water to a place which would otherwise be dry.

Mirage An optical illusion caused by light being bent by the layer of hot air above the desert..

Nocturnal Nocturnal animals come out at night; they sleep during the day.

Nomads People who wander from place to place, in search of food and water for themselves and their animals. They never settle in one place for long.

Oasis A rare fertile spot and source of water in the area.

Rain shadow An area on the sheltered side of a mountain which gets little rain.

Reg Arabic word for stony desert.

Sand Minute pieces of rock which have been worn down by the wind and weather.

Wadi A river bed in the desert which is usually dried up.

INDEX